10 Ways To Make Money With Just Dial

Deepak Yadav

ISBN 978-93-5667-071-6

© Deepak Yadav 2022

Published in India 2022 by Pencil

A brand of

One Point Six Technologies Pvt. Ltd.

123, Building J2, Shram Seva Premises,

Wadala Truck Terminal, Wadala (E)

Mumbai 400037, Maharashtra, INDIA

E connect@thepencilapp.com

W www.thepencilapp.com

All rights reserved worldwide

DISCLAIMER: *The opinions expressed in this book are those of the authors and do not purport to reflect the views of the Publisher.*

Author biography

I am an infopreneur and I make money online.

I have seen many ups and downs in my life.

But the year 2016 was the worst time of my life because at this time I was suffering from depression and anxiety.

I tried my best to get out of this mental state.

Today I am far away from depression and anxiety.

Actually, my life changed after the depression.

I learned many lessons from online learning during this time and I want to teach this lesson to you through my books.

I hope you get to learn a lot from my books about online earning which can change your career and life forever.

CONTENTS

1. Investing in the Share Market.................................15

2. By becoming a whole seller................................20

3. Data Entry Jobs 23

4. Transport Service..27

5.Becoming a Customer Executive 31

6.By becoming a tutor 34

7. Becoming a Web Developer 38

8.becoming a health advisor...............................42

9.By freelancing...45

10. By selling your service...................................48

Conclusion 51

Introduction

In today's fast-paced life, where technology is also increasing continuously, our work is becoming easier in the same way.

We have got new opportunities for development, but at the same time we have also got such facilities, using which all facilities can be obtained sitting at home.

Whether it is education or entertainment or service related to any other field, all can be obtained within few minutes.

If you have a smartphone or computer in your hand and you have a good knowledge of technology, then you can do all the work by typing on your smartphone while sitting at home using it.

Earning the same money has also become so easy that maximum profit can be earned through your passion and skill.

Not only this, such technology has also become available to grow your business, which can give recognition to your business from any corner of the world and you can illuminate the name of your business to any corner of the world.

In this book, we have told how you can grow your business using an online platform.

Here we are telling about a platform that has provided the facility of promoting business at the fingertips only.

Do you want to know which platform is that?

So to get the answer of this question, read this book till the end so that you can take advantage of every service of this platform.

Here we are going to tell you about this platform in detail, knowing about which you will be surprised that after a few minutes of work, your business will start growing and it will reach every corner of the world.

Hope you are curious to know about this platform.

We are talking about Just Dial.

Have you ever heard its name?

Somewhere it is not that you have heard its name but you do not know what it is and how it works?

So don't worry, here you will get answers to your questions.

The way to earn money through this platform is very easy but before going about how to earn money, we need to know what is Just Dial and how it works.

So let's know what is Just Dial?
What is Just Dial?

Just as Google is a search engine and we get all the information according to our mind, similarly Just Dial is also a search engine, through which you can get whatever information you want.

Just Dial is 1 Indian company with its head quarter located in Maharashtra and this company was started in 1996.

This company was established as a local search engine and now this company has become so popular that it is doing business with many countries.

This company provides service to the people through telephone service.

Suppose you want to know about a place, then you can use it to know where that place is and how far it is from your location.

Not only this, there are such features under this platform, using which you can get many facilities, no matter where you are.

To know about this, we will tell you in detail how this platform can be useful for us and also you are going to know some important things related to it here.

Let us know in simple words how Just Dial works-

Just Dial is a telephone service where you can get service through your phone as per your convenience.

To get the service of Just Dial, its app will also be available on the Play Store, by downloading which you can get all the information.

You will also find the Just Dial website on social media, so in this way you can connect to the Just Dial platform from any place.

Under Just Dial, you will find many categories from which you can get different types of information and know about the related market such as shopping malls, medical stores, travel, jobs and many more.

You can get information about all the types of information available under all these categories by just making a call.

If you want to contact Just Dial service, then you can call on its contact number 8888888888 or you can also use Just Dial app.

If we talk about the service available on Just Dial, then here we get many types of services like search, b2b, online shopping and many more, which makes it easy to stay connected with the market.

It is definitely a local search engine but it is quite trustworthy, so many people also like it.

You want to know what is the biggest feature of this platform?

So let us tell- the biggest feature of this platform is that here you can register your business.

This means that you can get in touch with your customer through just one phone call and once your business is registered on this platform, then there will be some people who visit this platform who will definitely take advantage of your service. Would like to raise money, so this is one of the best platforms to earn money.

Don't be surprised to know that with just one phone call your business can reach people, but it is true.

If you also want to take advantage of this facility and register your business, then next we are going to tell you how to do business registration in Just Dial.

So let's know-

2.How to do business registration in Just Dial?

If you also want to take your business to the people by using Just Dial's service, then first of all you have to register your business in Just Dial, for which the steps are very easy.

Here in very simple words, the process of business registration is being told for you in Just Dial, just follow it and in no time your business will be registered-

1. First you have to download the Just Dial app or you can also login by visiting its website.

2. When you download this app or login to its website then you have to go to its menu option.

3. Under the menu option you will see an option - List your Business.

4. By clicking on this option, you will see that many categories will appear in front of you, in which after selecting your business category, you will be asked some business details, such as-

Company Name - Here you have to write the name of your business or company like if you are opening a restaurant then write its name.

City - You have to write the name of the city in which you run your business.

Contact Person - Any visitor who wants to take your service has to call on your number, then here you have to write the name of the person who will receive the customer's call.

Mobile Number - Here you have to give your mobile number.

Landline Number - If your business has a landline number, then you have to enter it.

Area- In which area of the city you are running the business, you have to give information about it.

Pin Code - You have to enter the pin code of your area.

5. After doing this, the option of Continue will come in front of you, after clicking on which the process of business registration will be completed.

The thing to note here is that your business will be registered after 24 hours of applying for registration.

An SMS will come from the Just Dial company on your mobile number, as well as the Just Dial company will also call you and ask some questions for confirmation, after which you will get the approval after answering correctly and your business will be registered.

Isn't it the easiest way?

Hopefully, here you have easily understood how it works, but it is not limited to this, there are many other facilities available inside it.

After registering your business, you can also apply for any registration plan from this company.

Here you get two types of registration plans, one is paid registration and the other is free registration.

There is a slight difference between the two, so let us know what is the registration plan and what facilities are available under it-

3. Just Dial Registration Plans

Within the Just Dial registration, you get some registration plans, in which different charges have been determined according to the four types of plans.

Let's find out what is this after all?

Paid Registration

Under paid registration, you have to pay some charges for business registration, which is available in 3 types of packages and it provides some different facilities-

1. Diamond Package

Diamond package is the first package under pet registration.

Under this plan, if you register your business, then your business is on the top position on Just Dial, but a condition has been laid for this that this package is given to only one type of organizer of one business category and the rest It is also much more expensive than a plane.

2. Gold Package

The second paid registration plan is the Gold package, under which even if you register your business, you can still charge and this package is given to 10 to 20 organizers of the same category, but one advantage is available here that after the diamond package. This is the second expensive package i.e. cheaper than the Diamond package.

3.Silver Package

Now if we talk about silver package, then it is available after gold package, under which 10 to 20 organizers who do business of same category are given to them.

It is slightly cheaper than both the earlier packages.

Free Registration

Now it comes to free registration, under which there are no charges for doing business registration.

When you login by visiting its official website or download its app and register under this plan, then you can register for absolutely free, while if you want, just dial about these plans by calling the company's contact number. You can get complete information about this.

This has become the business registration and the necessary things related to its plan.

But the most important thing is that how can Just Dial be used in your business and how to grow your business here?

How can make him famous all over the world to earn maximum profit?

Here we have brought you 10 easy ways to earn money from Just Dial, using which you can earn maximum profit.

These are such methods that you have heard or read somewhere before but there will be very few people who will know that these methods can also be reached through the Just Dial platform and earn money by giving the best service. can.

So let's know what are 10 ways to earn money from Just Dial without wasting your time?

1. Investing in the Share Market

Who does not know the name of share market because it is such a path where once you have made your position then you will keep on moving forward.

You must have often heard people say that money is wasted in the stock market, so this is not the right way to earn money, but this is not completely true.

There are many billionaires in the world who have achieved such a high position by investing in the stock market, if they also thought that only money is wasted in the stock market, then they would never have reached this position.

So it is not fair to say that share market is not the right way to earn money but you can definitely say that it is not right to invest money on any shares without thinking.

There is a risk to invest in the share market because it cannot be said when the shares of which company will fall and which will rise, but if you analyze and invest in the right company, then no one can stop you from getting success.

One such company is Just Dial in which if you invest in the stock market then you have a lot of chances to get profit because if you see the position of the stock market of Just Dial company then you will be able to see very well how much growth it is also doing.

Keeping this in mind, investing in Just Dial's stock market can prove to be very beneficial.

If we talk about a recent report, then it is known that this year has been very good for Just Dial company because this year the shares of Just Dial's company have jumped 84% in a single month and it has the potential for even more growth. Is.

Not only this, in the quarter till September 30, 140 million users have been added to this company and 1 lakh paid subscribers have been added by this company.

Looking at these figures, it can be said that how much trustworthy this company is becoming and is worth investing in the stock market, so if you invest considering the position of the stock market of this company, then you will be investing in a very short time. I can increase my money manifold.

However, for this you have to have some patience because many times it happens that even after a long time, not much movement is visible, so after choosing the right company, you will have to give some time to the stock market.

If we talk about those shares of Just Dial which are most popular and growing a lot, then the business to business platform JD Mart has gained a lot under it.

Ever since the lockdown happened due to Corona virus, people's inclination towards e-commerce website increased a lot.

At that time people were doing more work of online shopping and online investing, during this time the shares of Just Dial Company saw a lot of boom and since then this company is touching the heights.

It is growing so fast that on 1st April the price of its one share was Rs 293 whereas now the price of its 1 share has gone up to Rs 682.

It is very easy to guess from this how much profit you can get here by investing in the stock market.

For business to business platform JD Mart, USB has set a budget of $15 million which is to be used to promote this platform.

The biggest news is that this platform is going to become the second largest platform in the market and it is expected to grow even more by 2025 where its share price is estimated at Rs 800.

On the other hand, if we talk about the biggest company competing in the business to business market, which has kept its foot on its first position, that is Indiamart.

This company has jumped 158% in the financial year and it is expected to grow even more in the coming time, between 2019 and 2022, this company has got a lot of profit.

One and a half lakh subscribers are associated with this company and are constantly taking advantage due to the increase in its share price, so if you also want to become one of them, then after analysis, join this company and earn money by investing in the stock market. can.

To compete with this company and earn more profits, Just Dial is constantly making new efforts, which are proving to be beneficial.

So in this way, if you invest in Just Dial's company under the share market, then it can prove to be a much better deal for you.

Once you buy a share, if its share price increases, then you get more profit and you do not have to work too hard to invest.

You can get all this information by calling the company of Just Dial.

This business to business platform is proving to be a great way to earn money from the share market.

So if you have already made up your mind to invest in the stock market and are looking for a company that can give you maximum returns, then you can think of investing in the Just Deal share market.

2. By becoming a whole seller

Household products used in homes are the biggest need of the people such as ration without which no one can live.

At the same time, everywhere you will also find shops of goods related to household products.

There are many shops where you get all the things you need at one place, which is called wholesale, not only this, but you can also get things in bulk and you know about all these things very well. And if you have a wholesale business, then you will know better about it that how important this work is for the people, so the earning is also high in the wholesaler.

The problem of many wholesalers is that their business runs only in their locality or their area, due to which they do not get much profit.

Are you one of them too?

If yes, then the solution to your problem is hidden in this book.

There are many ways that will help you to grow your business but some of these methods take a lot of time but there is one way which is very easy and can give you better results in less time.

That way is registration of wholesale business in Just Dial.

Yes, you read it right, by registering your business on this company, you will have chances of getting more profit from wholesale business and will be able to earn more.

For this, you just have to register your business and keep all the necessary things related to it in front of the people.

You have already been given information about how to register your business in Just Dial, you can upload your own catalog by following its steps.

Under Just Dial, you will get all the features that will help you in taking your business forward, such as you can write the description of the items you are selling under your business and can tell about your stock such as How is your business different from the rest of the business and what items will you make available to the people.

Apart from this, you can also upload their images, which will make it easier for people to buy goods.

Your mobile number is registered here, so the customer who needs your service will definitely contact you and the better you keep your business in front of people, the more benefit you will get.

The most important thing is that your catalog attracts them to you, so take care of good quality and price.

Once your customer likes your work then he becomes your customer forever.

But here you have to try to be as active as possible so that you can get in touch with all your customers and you can deliver items to them according to their needs.

In this way, you can easily earn money from Just Dial by becoming a wholesaler and if you are starting your business then this is a very good way for you to promote your business.

3. Data Entry Jobs

Did you know that you can also get a data entry job on the Just Dial platform?

No? So let's know about it in detail?

Often many companies keep taking out data entry job vacancies, you must have also heard about it.

But do you know what is a data entry job and where can you apply for it?

If not, then here you will get the answers to the questions related to them.

We also understand that the number of people who have never heard about data entry jobs will not be able to take advantage of it, if you are also one of them and reading about data entry for the first time. If so, then this book can prove to be very beneficial for you because here we are, what is a data entry job? And which is the best medium to apply for it? They are going to talk.

First of all you need to know what is a data entry job?

Data entry is a very easy job which can be done by students and housewives and this work can be done by managing the time of their own free will and if you want you can do this work full time or part time also.

Data entry is such a work under which you have to join a company and enter the data given by it and give it to the concerned company, where data entry means that you have to save the given information in the form of data and it The work has to be done in software like MS Word, MS Excel or Notepad.

Under this work, you will get many types of information which you will have to enter in the website of the company.

Now you must be thinking that which companies take out such job vacancies?

So there are many private companies or government offices that offer such jobs.

You may be asked to enter the full details of the employees of the company and many other types of data may be given to you.

The best thing is that it does not require much technology knowledge, if you have basic knowledge of internet then you can do this work easily.

Many tasks like filling online forms, entering captcha, entering captions, converting audio to text, processing emails come under data entry in which you can work according to your convenience.

Now you must have understood what is data entry but the question comes that where to apply for data entry job or through which platform to reach your profile to the people where you can get a chance to earn maximum money?

The answer is Just Dial.

When you search under Just Dial Company, you will find that there are many data entry job vacancies available in which you can get a job by just one call and not just one but you can do this work for many people simultaneously.

This method of earning money in Just Dial is very popular because data entry jobs are easily available here.

Here you will find many people who must have listed the vacancy of data entry job in their business as well as this is a job that you will not lack, so if you have ever done data entry work before or you are new in this field. So you can reach people through Just Dial by creating your service profile i.e. registering your work.

You can publish your contact number by creating your profile in Just Dial so that whenever someone searches for data entry job on Just Dial, your profile will be the first to see them and they can contact you.

Even if you do not have experience in this work, you will not face any kind of problem because as you go on doing this work, your skills will improve.

But you also need to be a little careful here because due to the popularity of Just Dial's company, many such people are also present here who take wrong advantage of it because they know that this kind of work is being done on this platform. There will be many people for it.

These people get the data entry work done but do not pay for it, so before working for anyone, you have to investigate about them.

Whenever you get a call from someone or whenever you contact someone, then get to know about them well and only then start working for them.

In this way, you can earn a lot of money even by doing data entry job on Just Dial because in this work less effort and more profit is available.

Also, you can register your service absolutely free in dial soon, so you will not be at risk of any loss, so you can work here with rest and earn money.

4. Transport Service

You must know about the transport service, you will find many options under the transport service in our country because many transport services are used here for the import and export of goods.

If you also want to take advantage and earn money through transport service, then this can prove to be a good option for you.

But it is important to know about what is a transport service, only then you will be able to take the right advantage of it.

To start a transport service, you will have to invest some money in the beginning because it is a business that has to be registered legally before starting, which is done by the central government and when you register your business. If you do, you will get ShopAct License, Udyog Aadhaar and GST Number.

After registering, you have to use Just Dial, as you know Just Dial is a local search engine where the people of the city take information about many types of service through telephone service and use it.

When you get the transport firm registered on behalf of the central government, then you will have to register it on Just Dial because here your business can get a lot of benefits.

After this, the most important thing is to get the transport code from the logistics companies of the city, which is necessary for the transport service.

If you do not want to open a transport firm, then no problem, the option of transport service is not limited to this only and there are many other options to earn money from here.

You get many more options under this service, as there is another important and popular service which is used by every person today and that is taxi service.

This business is going on a lot today and its popularity has increased even today because today taxi service can be availed by just making a call or through the app.

Wherever people want to go, they can book Ola and Uber taxis using their smartphone and it saves their time too.

If you have a car or a taxi, then you can use it in this business, here it is not necessary that you use only one car in this business, you can put many cars in this business. and can earn money.

All you have to do is register your taxis and cars on Just Dial from where some customer will definitely contact you to take advantage of your taxi service.

Under Transport Service, we tell you another way by which you can earn a lot of money through Just Dial and that is the business of taking car on rent which is very famous in India.

People who do not have a car and do not want to use public vehicles, such people prefer to rent a car when they have to cover a long distance, then there is an increased possibility that they also want to rent a car. Use a search engine like Just Dial.

Therefore, if you want, you can also make it your business and take money from your customer according to the distance, from which a good amount of income can be obtained.

Often, even during marriage or any other function, the work of booking vehicles starts getting more and the earning is also very high during this period.

You can rent your car and get paid on hourly and day-by-day basis.

Apart from these options, there are many options that you can use under transport service such as cold chain service, logistics company, luxury bus rental, packers and movers etc.

In this way, earning money from Just Dial Transport Service is also very beneficial, so if you already drive a taxi or rent a car or you have a transport firm which is not doing well then you can register it on Just Dial. Due to which your business will start growing.

With the help of this local search engine, you connect with more and more people and this becomes the reason for earning your profit.

5. Becoming a Customer Executive

Just Dial Company not only gives a chance to register business, but it is a company that also removes job vacancies from time to time in which if you have all the skills and eligibility which the company has decided then you too under this company. can get job.

One such job is customer care executive.

But before getting its job, it is important to know that what is a customer executive and what is his job?

So let us tell you here what type of job it is-

Customer care executive means to give complete information related to any service and try to solve the problems of the people like you have often seen that if any electronic item in your house gets damaged and when you contact its concerned company If you do, then the people of that company try to fix that item and solve your problems, they are called customer care executives.

For example, suppose you have recharge in your mobile but outgoing service of your mobile is not working or internet is not working then you will contact your respective sim card company with whom you will share your problems and they will solve it to you.

Just the same work has to be done under the customer care executive job, Just Dial's company keeps on taking out this type of job vacancy if you are interested in this type of work and can do this work easily and can handle the customer. This job is just for you.

To get this job in Just Dial's company, you will have to give an interview where you will be asked many questions along with your communication skills, if you pass this interview then you will get a job in this company very easily. .

There are many job posts in which there are interviews in three to four rounds, so you have to be prepared for all kinds of interview sessions.

You can get all the information related to this job by just dialing the company's contact number and you can apply for this job according to the eligibility.

If you get a job here, then you will have to try to solve the problems of the people by becoming a customer care expert and at the same time make them aware of all the services of Just Dial from time to time.

If we talk about the salary of this post, then from the very beginning you get a good salary for it, which gradually increases with time.

According to an average, the salary of a Just Dial customer care executive is about two lakh rupees annually, that is, he gets a salary of 15 thousand to 16 thousand rupees every month, so if you are interested in this work and the customers inside you If you have the ability to handle and listen to their problem and try to solve it, then you will be able to do this work very easily and will also be able to earn a lot of money.

A customer service executive plays a huge role in a company as they generate leads and manage the team.

Communicating with the customer, understanding their needs and delivering the right information to them, it is a very responsible job, so if you can do all these things then only you should apply for this job.

So in this way, you can earn a lot of money by directly joining the company of Just Dial because the rate of Just Dial company is very good, so working by joining it can be very beneficial for you.

The staff of this company is also very friendly, so working with it can be a good experience for you.

The staff associated with this also believes that Just Dial Company has proved to be a good platform to start your career, so you should also start working from here.

6.By becoming a tutor

Internet is not lagging behind in any field today, it has also played an important role in the field of education.

Most of the students are getting education only through the internet, whereas the students whether they want to get any information or prepare for any project related to their school, internet is being used in every work.

It can be understood from this that the Internet has an important role in both online education or offline.

This era of online education has also played an important role in maintaining the future of the children.

Most of the students are getting education only through the internet, whereas the students whether they want to get any information or prepare for any project related to their school, internet is being used in every work.

It can be understood from this that the Internet has an important role in both online education or offline.

This era of online education has also played an important role in maintaining the future of the children.

While the havoc of Corona was wreaking havoc all over the world, students were getting education only through online education.

During this time, more importance has been given to education.

But nowadays students and their parents are worried that they are not getting good teachers who give good education, due to which the future of the student is in danger.

That's why they also keep trying to hire a good teacher through online medium as much as possible.

If you want to make a career in this field keeping this in mind, then you can earn a lot of money and the best thing in this is that if you want, you can work as a tutor both online or offline and this It is also very beneficial.

But the problem is where should we start and where will we get more and more students for our class?

So let us tell you that in Just Dial also you can promote your service among the people by registering your tutor work.

If you get a call from someone who lives near your area, then you can also do tutor work offline, where you can go to their home and teach the student or you can go to their nearby area. You can start a tutoring class in your own home by gathering more children.

On the other hand, if such people contact you who do not live in your area ie live from your city, then you can arrange online education for them.

It is very easy to register your business in Just Dial, as you know, so if you search there in this category, then you will see that many people are associated with this work in the same way.

If like them, you also want to earn money by giving education, then you can also apply for online class or offline class by registering your work on Just Dial and earn a lot of money.

If you have the skill to teach something to people, then this work of yours can go on for a long time and it is not necessary that you should teach only small children of school, if you want to teach high school, college students and adult people. You can also educate, for this you just need to have a good knowledge of the related subject.

It is also good to start tutor work using Just Dial because here you are not asked any kind of experience.

Even if you do not have experience at all and you are completely new in this field, then you can do this work very easily.

Here the more students and their parents like your method of teaching, the more your business will grow.

At the same time, you will start getting calls from more people and you know why this work becomes even easier in Just Dial because if you want, you can attract people towards you by making your profile made in Just Dial more attractive. For example, when you write the name of your educational institution in the name of your company, then also write some of its characteristics there such as what subjects your class is popular for etc.

In this way, starting a tutor job on Just Dial can also prove to be much easier and more rewarding.

Here you will easily find students and if you want, you can get information from those people who are already associated with this field, so if you are thinking of starting the work of expansion of education, then once you just dial But you should definitely see this work by promoting it, it may accelerate your work so much that you have not even imagined.

7. Becoming a Web Developer

Web developer means the developer of a website.

You must have heard about it and if you have not heard it, then now know what it is and how much you can earn by doing this work.

You must know that this is the age of the Internet and the work of making websites under the Internet has increased a lot.

Their importance has increased so much that today students are also being given web development courses so that they can walk step by step with the world.

But what is this web developer after all?

Let's know-

Developing any website and making it well controlled is the job of a web developer, simply managing a website is web development.

Web developers keep on making some changes to their website from time to time according to the demand of the customer and get paid handsomely in return.

But the job of a web developer is not that easy, for this you should have creativity, passion and skill.

If you have communication skills and are able to work with a team and at the same time you have all the information about the technology related to it, then you can also work as a web developer.

There are some important things inside this work that you have to take care of, such as coding and related languages, without which the work of web development cannot be done well.

It is true that now the technology has increased so much that you will also find such applications in which you can do the work of developer without coding, but coding is a very important component for the security of the website, so its information is necessary.

If you are a web developer and you have done some courses related to it and you are worried that you do not have much project due to which you are not able to earn profit then the solution of your problem is in this book and that is - Just Dial.

As you have already read that Just Dial is a popular and trusted platform and how it helps to grow your business, then by adopting this method, you too can get the project from your client.

When you register your business on Just Dial, your chances of getting clients are very high.

Due to being a popular platform, after Google, most people search on Just Dial to get their favorite service and here it is very easy to get many results in a single search, so these chances increase even more. It is that your business will also come in front of people and there will definitely be some people who will contact you.

The work of a web developer is such that there will be no shortage in the future because now every person is launching his own website where there is a need to develop the website from time to time.

On the other hand, if people need a creative web developer, then it is obvious that they will search online only on platforms like Google or Just Dial.

Therefore, when you register your web developer business on Just Dial, your chances of getting the benefits increase even more.

This field is so spread that if you want, you can get this type of job in foreign countries where you can do this work either full time or part time.

There is also a convenience here that if you do not register your business on Just Dial and try to contact those people on Just Dial who take out such job vacancy, you can still benefit.

Many times it happens that if a client is not coming to you then you have to go to the client, it is not a bad thing, so if you contact such people on Just Dial, then you will get a good job in any company. If you go, then at the beginning of your career, you can earn 30 thousand to 35 thousand rupees a month.

If you do not want to do full time job in any company and want to do this work as a freelancer i.e. want to get your payment after completing the project by working independently, then you can also do this work so web developer Making a career by becoming one is a very good option and Just Dial makes this task even easier.

8.becoming a health advisor

Who does not care about his health in this fast moving world?

Some are concerned about their increasing weight, some are concerned about their decreasing weight, some have problems with sleep, some have physical pain and sometimes these conditions become even more serious, after which people have to consult a health advisor. There is no choice but to talk.

A health advisor is someone who listens to the health problems of the people and tells them the remedies.

If you have information related to this field and you can make people aware of health, then you can become a good health advisor from which you can earn a lot of money.

In this fast-paced life, people do not have enough time to take care of their health, in such a situation, new diseases keep taking birth which becomes a big problem in future.

In such a situation, if you reduce the problems of people by becoming a health advisor and try to overcome their problems, then you can help them as well as help yourself.

On Just Dial, you also get the option to register a business related to the health category where you can work as a health advisor.

As we mentioned that people are showing a lot of interest in Just Dial and search on the platform to get all kinds of service, similarly they may also use Just Dial to get health related advice.

When you search under this category, you will be able to see how many people are joining the medical field and working as health advisors and if you also want to be one of them and want to earn a lot then it is better for you. There may be an option.

On the other hand, if we talk about what advice you can give to people under Health Advisor, then under this you can share information related to food and how to keep your routine balanced etc.

All of you are aware that ever since the outbreak of Corona has spread in the world, many health related diseases are flourishing in our country and everyone from children to elders is facing some health related difficulties. .

Therefore, in the present times, providing correct information to the people by working as a health advisor can prove beneficial not only for them but also for you.

If you want, you can also connect with any medical institution through Just Dial and work as a health advisor from there.

If you run your own private organization and want it to benefit you as much as possible, then you can register your business on Just Dial and promote it to the people.

So in this way, Health Advisor is also a good way to earn money, through which you can register in Just Dial company and reach your facility to the people and in return you can get a good payment.

The work of a health advisor is a prestigious job, for which you should have the right information related to this field, only then your business will be able to run well.

The more you stay in touch with your patient, the more profit you will get.

9.By freelancing

In today's digital age, who would not have heard the name of freelancer work, freelancing means earning money by working independently.

There are many people who do not like to do jobs because they do not like to work under someone and they want to start a job in which they are their own boss.

That's why these people take the path of freelancing because in this work you get the opportunity that you can do any work anytime you want by managing time and earn money in return.

But did you know that you can also work as a freelancer in Just Dial?

If you register your freelancing work with Just Dial company, then your chances of getting new projects will increase a lot.

We will tell you about that in a little detail, but first know what works you can do under freelancing.

Freelancing is a contract best business in which you take a project from a company or an individual and get paid by completing it.

Within freelancing work you can do many tasks like video editing, translation, app developer, graphic design, logo design, content writing and for this work you only need laptop, mobile or computer which is well connected to internet connection .

If you have freelancing skills then you can easily earn a lot of money in less time.

Here you can also do tasks like virtual assistant and social media marketing.

On Just Dial you will find many such people who will be seen doing such kind of work and if you also want to earn money by becoming one of them then this can provide you a good opportunity.

As you know that people keep searching for freelancing work like web developer on Just Dial, then it can happen in the same way people also use Just Dial for other freelancing work, so you can register your work on this platform. You can give this business a chance so that it can grow.

Now the demand of freelancer in the market has increased a lot because everyone is engaged in digital marketing today, some are opening a website and some are becoming a part of social media marketing, for which they often need freelancers from time to time. Is.

In such a situation, if someone contacts you under Just Dial and he likes your work, then you can work for them permanently and even after that, if you do not want to do any permanent work, then still your career in this field. can make.

In this way Just Dial provides you opportunities to earn money by freelancing too.

10. By selling your service

As far as you came to know how to earn money by registering your business with Just Dial, but apart from these, there is a way in Just Dial by which you can earn money and that is to earn money by selling your service.

You know how to register your business on Just Dial, when you complete this process, you become a seller in Just Dial in which you can sell any of your services.

Just Dial gives you the insurance that your business will come in front of more and more customers on this platform, thereby giving you opportunities to make profits.

You will get many options inside selling your service like if you are creative then you can sell it by making handmade things where there is very little investment and by putting catalog in just dial you can promote it more and more. Huh.

One such hand made business is the business of making candles which is very popular because candles or lamps are needed in every festival and worship.

In such a situation, if you do the work of providing this kind of service to the people, then where people will easily get the goods of their needs, there will be chances of getting maximum profits.

This is a work that takes very little money and there is a lot of scope for this business to grow in the future.

Whenever the thought of decorating the house comes in the mind of the people, the first thing that comes to their mind is the candles.

Apart from this, you can also earn money by promoting the business of others on Just Dial, such as suppose that there is a business near you whose service is not reaching the people, then you can contact those people for their business. You can take some charges by registering on Just Dial.

This is also a good way to earn money because those whose business is not running, they will be ready to give you money to run their business, so if you take 100 rupees from one person for this work and 10 people in a day. If you register your business then you can earn 1000 rupees in a day by doing a little hard work.

Also you can do this work that you help in selling other's service where you can get commission on every product sale.

Now running own business has become very common and in all this, every person wants to use digital tools so that his business can grow more and more without much effort, hence the methods used to sell the product earlier.

They are also slowly dying out and the traditional business is being replaced by digital business.

Meanwhile, Just Dial has also gained a lot of popularity where it has helped people to reach their target customers with ease.

So if you also want to sell any of your services on Just Dial, then quickly register on this platform and see how great results this platform gives you and how your small business also earns a big name.

Conclusion

So you saw how today's increasing technology has made everything easier.

But did you think that using Just Dial you can get so many great service or join this company and benefit by growing the business through its best features?

As technology is increasing, the work has become much easier, at the same time this world of mobile and computer has provided us with so many comforts by connecting us with digital marketing that now no task can be called impossible. can.

By pressing just a few buttons, you can get rid of all your problems.

The features of Just Dial have given people better results in a very short span of time, due to which their business is at great heights today and still those people are using this platform to get even more profits.

If you also want to reach the heights by becoming one of those people and want to make all your dreams come true then Just Dial platform can be the beginning of a good career for you.

Talking about the Indian industry's company Just Dial, recently some facts related to it are coming out in which it is being said that Mukesh Ambani's Reliance Company wants to buy Just Dial Company, although it is difficult to say that it is. The news is true or not.

During this, questions started arising in the minds of people that what is Just Dial? And how does it work?

This company has made a very good place among the people in a very short time, if we talk about its initial phase, then when this company started then only 5 employees were associated with this company and only to launch it. 50 thousand rupees, but when this company launched its website in 2007, then this company has become very popular and started expanding a lot.

Since then till date this company is providing facilities to the people which can be availed with the help of telephone.

There are many such features under Just Dial, by using which it has become very easy to reach the business to the people, so if you also register your business with this company, then the chances of expanding your business increase a lot.

Whatever the platform, if you want to earn money, then you have to be patient because you know very well that no work can be done overnight, for this you have to give some time to your business.

So do not think that as soon as you register in this company, you will start getting calls from customers or you will start getting profits.

But have faith that you can earn a lot of money by using this platform.

All the visitors who use this app and trust Just Dial's company, there will definitely be some who would like to take advantage of your service and call you, so be patient and try to do whatever facilities you can through the company. He is unique when he reaches out to the people.

Because unless a customer sees the features of your service, he will not have a reason to use your service, so try to bring a unique service to the people.

Nowadays, the number of people working in each field has become very high, so it becomes even more important that you do something different from other people so that your customers can be attracted towards you.

Hope you like our book and help you take advantage of Just Dial's company facilities.

If you want to get new and accurate information like this, then stay connected with us continuously.